A Question of Timing:
Successful Men Talk About Having Children

Having children too soon can make it difficult for young parents to accomplish their own goals.

The Teen Pregnancy Prevention Library

A Question of Timing:

Successful Men Talk About Having Children

by Barbara Moe

THE ROSEN PUBLISHING GROUP, INC.
NEW YORK

Published in 1997 by The Rosen Publishing Group, Inc.
29 East 21st Street, New York, NY 10010

First Edition

Library of Congress Cataloging-in-Publication Data

Moe, Barbara A.
    A question of timing : successful men talk about having children /
by Barbara Moe.
      p.   cm. — (The teen pregnancy prevention library)
    Includes bibliographical references and index.
    Summary: Young men discuss how delaying or deciding against
fatherhood has allowed them to accomplish career and personal goals.
    ISBN 0-8239-2253-7
    1. Family size—United States—Juvenile literature.
  2. Childlessness—United States—Juvenile literature.
  3. Fatherhood—United States—Juvenile literature.
[1. Childlessness. 2. Family life.] I. Title. II. Series.
HQ762.U6M64 1997
306.874′2—dc20   95-42470
                                         CIP
                                         AC

Manufactured in the United States of America

Contents

Introduction

YOUNG PEOPLE WITH GOALS AND DREAMS FOR THE future are more likely to postpone having children than those who see their future as bleak. In this book, we will hear from ten men who did not become fathers as teenagers. They decided to wait and go after their dreams.

Teen fathers are an important part of the teen pregnancy problem. Here are some facts about young fathers:

- The fathers of the children born to teen moms are usually twenty-five years of age or younger.
- Many young fathers cannot make enough money to support a family.
- Sixty percent of teenage families live in poverty.
- Young fathers often don't stick around. A recent study tells us that 85 percent of the fathers of babies born to teen moms do not live with and are not involved in the lives of the child and mother.

Teenage fathers (compared with nonfathers

Eighty-five percent of teen fathers do not take an active role in their children's lives.

of the same age) are more likely to drop out of high school. An organization called Advocates for Youth says that only 39 percent of teen fathers get their high school certifications by age twenty. Compare this with the 86 percent certification rate of men who do not become young fathers. In addition, teenage fathers are only half as likely to finish college as young males of the same age who delay fatherhood. Statistics show that college graduates earn about 40 percent more money in their lifetimes than those with only a high school education.

Many young men have a hard time supporting themselves. Add a wife or girlfriend and a child, and the going can get really tough. Most young fathers are not ready for this kind of responsibility. And studies indicate that young parents are more likely than older parents to abuse or neglect their children.

We call the young men you will meet in this book "successful." By successful, we mean that they are working to reach educational goals, career goals, or personal goals. They are of different ethnic backgrounds and religions. Some are well-off. Others make just enough money to get by. They talk about their reasons for waiting to have children. Some are still single, while others are married but have chosen not to have kids yet—or ever. Two have children, but waited until they were really ready.

These men describe in their own words what their families were like when they were growing up. Some of them had a lot of help from their families. Others did not. Some had support or inspiration from an important person outside their family. This person—often a teacher—helped them dream of a brighter future. Some of the young men talk about mistakes they made and how they learned from their mistakes. They also discuss their relationships, past and present. You will see that teen fatherhood *is* avoidable, no matter what one's background. And you will learn of the rewards of postponing fatherhood: having more time, energy, and resources to devote to your own hopes and dreams.

CLIFF WOULD LIKE TO BE A COLLEGE professor someday. Meanwhile he is making a living as an accountant. At twenty-nine, Cliff is not married, but he does have a serious girlfriend. Cliff and Susan recently started going to counseling together. They are learning about how their families have influenced their lives and their behaviors. Cliff talks about some of the stumbling blocks in his life, and how he continues to try to overcome them.

1 CLIFF— Self-Made Accountant

I'M THE LAST OF SIX KIDS. I CAN'T SAY I LIKE BEING the youngest. Even now, people in my family rarely take me seriously.

I was born in Morristown, New Jersey—a small town at that time. If you got in trouble, everybody knew it. My teen years were pretty wild. I did some crazy things like throwing snowballs at cars and lighting firecrackers—stuff like that. When something bad happened, the cops always came to our house first.

My childhood was happy, except that my father was an alcoholic. Nobody in the family will talk about the way things were. He was a nice guy, very loving, when he wasn't drinking. But if he'd been drinking, look out. We all walked on eggshells. We never knew on any given night what his mood would be.

My brother Matt, two years older, never disagreed with my father. He tried to make everything normal. He'd say, "Don't make waves." I was more willing to argue with Dad.

There were lots of good parts, though. We lived on a ten-acre farm for eighteen years. We vacationed on a lake in Canada. Because of those experiences, I developed a love of nature. We went hiking, camping, boating, and swimming. Also, being the youngest, I had a close relationship with my mother. She took the time to listen to me. And my sister Lexie, nine years older, seemed like a second mother.

At college I thought about career choices for the first time. I attended Queens University in Kingston, Ontario. Why there? Because they accepted me. My grades from high school weren't that great. My first year of college was rough. At the beginning of my sophomore year I realized that *I* was in control. No one else was going to do it for me. After that, I got mostly As. I graduated with a B.A. with honors in political science.

I planned to get a Ph.D. at the University of British Columbia and become a college professor. But to continue with school I needed financial help. As an American in Canada, I wasn't eligible. So I scrapped my original idea and moved back to the States.

I was desperate for work. I applied for a job as an accounts payable manager at a company. They said, "Do you know accounting?" I said I did even

With practice, a hobby can become a serious option for the future.

though I'd never taken an accounting course in my life. I learned as I went along. I'd say, "I just want to be sure I'm doing this your way." Then they'd show me. After three years, the company moved to California.

At that time I made a big mistake: I accepted an offer to start a business with my father and older brother. Our product was a three-dimensional art medium. To start a new business, you have to have confidence in yourself and your product. But my father and brother were negative. They discouraged everything I tried to do. I worked with them for three years, earning very little money. Finally I quit. The business failed. There were not many positives from that experience. But I did learn that I could work fourteen-hour days, seven days a week!

Now I'm trying to recover from the experience of working in a family company. I'm back in accounting at an engineering firm involved in tele-communications. The company is positive and forward-looking. It's fun to go to work.

I still have my dreams. One is to go back to school. But I may have to study business so my company will pay for it. My main hobby is music. At various times I write songs, play drums, and sing. I'd like to get a group together that could make money. I'd also love to go backpacking in Nepal and climb all the 14,000-foot peaks in Colorado. If I ever get enough money, I'll get a pilot's license. And someday I'd like to live out in the country.

I wouldn't have been a good father at twenty. You have to give up too much to be an effective parent at that age. It's a twenty-four-hour-a-day job. I have one friend who's forty. His first child is a year old now. Even at his age he struggles with the challenges of parenting. My girlfriend and I have been going together for almost five years, but we're not ready to have kids. I hope that by waiting I'll be a better father someday.

Fatherhood requires a strong sense of self-confidence and responsibility.

DUANE IS A TALL AND MUSCULAR MAN. AT forty, he keeps fit by swimming and lifting weights. He has worked in physical education his whole adult life. He likes his job so much that it doesn't seem like work. Duane has known his share of sorrow. First his mother died, then in the past year his twin brother, Darrell, passed on. Duane is deeply religious and writes poetry.

2 DUANE— Karate and Poetry

HERE ARE THE FINAL LINES FROM DUANE'S poem, *Nourishment*:

Look into your heart and see the beauty
   from within you, and let it grow.

For what good is it to gain the world and lose
   the soul,
you can't take it with you.

Let it out, be a free and happy spirit,
   giving love wherever you go.

Remember, in every living thing
   strives a spirit to be free.

That is why, when we look at the world,
   sometimes we cry.

Don't let anyone keep you from reaching for your dreams in sports or other activities for which you have talent.

I teach fitness courses, basketball, volleyball, tee-ball, weightlifting, swimming, crafts, and karate: the *art* of karate. That's quite a bit different from the sport of karate. The art of karate teaches confidence, respect, and discipline. It's fun to see the kids gain confidence—their grades improve, and they get along better with their peers. Sometimes their parents are so impressed that they join in.

I love working with people, but my first love is poetry. I write poems and then recite them at local churches. I have a book of poems that was published in 1973, and several of my poems are in national anthologies. My own church has performed one of my plays. It's a religious love story written in verse.

Although I'm a poet, I don't want to be a starving artist. A person needs a stable income. In college I majored in English. But I went back to school later and took management courses. My next move will be to a directorship of a recreation center.

A lot of people don't believe in goals and dreams, but I have big dreams. I'd like to make the Olympics in swimming—in the 50- or 100-meter freestyle or in the breaststroke. There's no support because they say I'm too old or that blacks can't swim well enough. Well, I've written a book about a new kind of training for swimmers. It's called *Fast Twitch Training*, and it's a special way of working with weights. This kind of training really helps me. Next week I'm going to be in a triathlon. I put together the team, and I'll do the swimming.

I don't always work and *work out*. I have a toy that I work *on*. It's a 1931 Chevy coupe, a hot rod with a V-8 engine and lots of chrome. I also like to go to the mountains to enjoy God's gift of nature. And I teach a Sunday school class of middle-school kids.

When I get married, I'd like to find someone with good morals, a person who would be support-ive of my dreams and goals. And I'd be supportive of *her* goals.

It is important for both partners in a couple to support each other's goals.

Sure, I'd like to get married. I know some of my goals will change. But they won't disappear completely. The advantage of being as old as I am is that you've reached a lot of your goals. I'm ready to concentrate on someone else. I wouldn't have been a good father at twenty because I lacked self-confidence. Older men make better fathers because they know who they are. What if my son asked me, "Dad, how do I reach a dream?" What if I had to say, "I don't know, I've never reached one."

When I was about eleven years old, I fell off the high board at the Y and landed on the concrete. I got a skull fracture and was in a coma for two days. The hardest thing I ever did was to climb up on that high board again. I learned that you never quit. You always do the best you can. That's what I'd like to teach my children.

PAUL HAS A THREE-YEAR-OLD, BUT IT'S NOT A child. It's a horse named Diamond Midnight. In addition to owning a racehorse, Paul is also a hockey player. Several years ago he and his father were talking about Wayne Gretzsky, the professional hockey star. Gretzsky had a horse that won a race in France. At that time in his life Paul began to think: I can do anything anyone else can do *at my own level*. For Paul, this philosophy of life means accepting himself. At thirty-one, he can challenge himself to reach his own potential. He can try new things. He can enjoy life, and he does.

3 PAUL— Owner of a Four-Legged Kid

I'M THE SECOND OF TWO BOYS IN MY FAMILY. MY brother Graham is thirty-four. He's an independent TV producer. My dad used to work in television, but now he works for a newspaper. My mom used to be a teacher, but now she inspects day-care facilities.

I had a happy childhood. But when I was twelve or thirteen, my parents got a divorce. I became rebellious and lost focus in my life. My grades suffered, and so did my hockey. I dropped out of school as a junior. The rebellious period lasted until I was about seventeen.

A major turning point for me was going to live with my mom. At that time she was teaching on a Navajo reservation in Arizona. While there, I took a look around. It didn't take long for me to realize all the opportunities I'd had that some people don't have. Six months later I moved back home with a new attitude. I wanted to make the most of my life. I re-enrolled in high school and graduated a year later at eighteen. During this time, I also worked for a Greek couple. They owned a restaurant, and they let me manage it at night. I had a taste of responsibility and got some experience.

Around this time I met a girl. Sandra was from Peru. We fell in love. I thought having her was all I needed. We went to see her family. Her dad wanted her to stay in Peru. The only way we could avoid that was to get married. We did. We were both nineteen.

Neither of us wanted to have kids. We were more concerned with our own lives and with what we needed and wanted to do. She wanted to become a lawyer, which she did in the nine years we were married. I worked my way up in hotel management and became a banquet manager. I worked at different restaurants, usually in hotels. I stayed about two years at each place—until I got bored. Finally, I opened my own restaurant in partnership with a friend. One thing I learned was that it's hard to mix business and friendship. I gained a new outlook on what I would do differently next time. I would have everything mapped out in advance.

We had a difference in philosophies. For one thing, he didn't want to spend money on advertising, and I did. After a year, I sold most of my shares to him. Now I'm a banquet manager in a big hotel again. Someday, when I get enough

Focusing on your responsibilities, such as schoolwork, can get you where you want to go in life.

money, I'd like to open a bed-and-breakfast place
or maybe a health food restaurant and bakery. I'd
like to own my own business again. But for now
this work is okay. My salary, working conditions,
and benefits are good.

I enjoy a lot of different things. My horse is a
big interest. I've always loved horses. When I was a
kid, my dad took me to the races a few times. The
whole atmosphere of the racetrack is exciting. I like
to watch the horses train, and it's fun to talk to the
jockeys. The people who work with the horses are
honest and decent. Many of the jockeys are very
religious.

The day I decided I wanted a horse, I also realized something else. I didn't have enough money

to buy a racehorse. But I could get a horse to breed. I looked at the ads in the paper, found a horse, and bought it. Unfortunately, that horse couldn't have foals. But the owners of the ranch wanted to help me achieve my goal. So they rented out a mare with free breeding to the stallion. That's how Diamond Midnight came to be born. I go to all the races. She's my baby. It's something like watching your child go off to kindergarten.

Hockey is another big interest of mine. I made a go of playing professional hockey. After three try-outs and one free agent camp, I realized I was probably too old. But I can still play for fun—on *my* level.

I like to go boating, hiking, and camping with my girlfriend. Camping is a challenge. You try to provide yourselves with a certain comfort level. This can be difficult, especially in the rain. Winter camping is something else. I even got a book from the library to learn how to build a snow cave. You spend twenty-four hours a day trying to stay warm. Sometimes it's good to push yourself to the limit.

Three years ago I met Martha, my girlfriend. We recently bought a house together. It's 108 years old and in a lower-income, blue-collar neighborhood. We consider ourselves married because we live together. That arrangement is fine with both of us. We share expenses, and she's the beneficiary of my life insurance. We might get a puppy, but right now we don't want to have kids. Most of my friends aren't married and don't have children. The only pressure I've gotten from anyone is from my mom. She would like to have another grandchild. She already has two, my brother's kids.

I wouldn't have been a good father at twenty. I was too reckless and too busy trying to figure out my own life. I would not have been a good influence on a young life. Both of us would have been messed up. Older people ought to be more grounded, have more direction, and make better parents.

Sometimes I wonder why anyone would want to bring up a child in this day and age. In many ways the future doesn't look very hopeful. But I'm already here, so I plan to enjoy life and explore the world.

KELVIN IS A YOUNG ATTORNEY (LAWYER). HE works for one of the largest law firms in his region. As a child, Kelvin didn't like going to church. Now, at twenty-seven, he goes willingly. He likes the adult Sunday school class. Here he gets ideas on how to apply religion to his daily life. He keeps in shape by participating in sports, especially football and basketball. For more than four years, he has had a pilot's license.

4 KELVIN— Law and Sunday School

I'M AN ONLY CHILD. MY FATHER WAS TWENTY YEARS old when I was born, and my mother was twenty-one. She finished her last two years of college after my birth. I lived with my grandparents for those two years. Both of my parents graduated from college. My mother's a teacher, and my father is a manager in the entertainment field.

I grew up in Alabama. In about eighth or ninth grade I started thinking about career choices. But I didn't decide on a law career until college. I went to Howard University in Washington, DC, and majored in microbiology and philosophy. Then I got a master's degree in philosophy, also at Howard.

During college, some friends and I decided to start a business. I became part owner of a restaurant. We specialized in gourmet chicken wings. Soon I started law school in Alabama, and our restaurant moved to Oklahoma. So I sold my part of the business.

I had a good childhood with supportive parents.

Marriage and family require commitment and a big investment of time and money.

My mother always said you can do anything you want to do if you work hard. But I never felt pressure to do a certain thing. In high school I worked a lot. Summers I'd have one or two jobs. I worked at a music store and a toy store.

I have strong memories of my grandfather. He worked in construction doing manual labor. I never saw him at his job, but I could see him going to work in his truck. At the end of the day when he came home, he was tired, but he'd do more work. He'd cut the grass or work on the cars. He didn't spend much money, and he didn't take many vacations.

I guess I have a lot of my grandfather in me. He

used to take my cousins and me out to a hamburger place called Jack's. He'd say, "Order whatever you want, but you better eat it all." To this day I don't like wasting food, maybe because of my grandfather's influence. I'm not a big spender like some of my friends. I used to hate to break a five-dollar or ten-dollar bill. Even now when I get my check from work, I keep a little out for expenses and put the rest in the bank.

My job, working with big companies, is interesting. Also, I started teaching classes in ethics and law at a local college. But I don't want to do the same thing forever. I'd like to own my own business and be totally in control.

I have a girlfriend, but I'm in no hurry to get married. I don't mind being alone some of the time. Still, I'd like to be a husband and father someday. It's fun to think of teaching a child and passing on knowledge.

In relationships some girls try to pressure you. They may want to get married so they can have kids. I try not to give in to that pressure. Most of my friends are still single. Of the married ones, only a few have kids.

I think I could have done a decent job of being a father at twenty, but I didn't want to. As a parent, you have to make too many sacrifices, and I wasn't ready.

DAVID IS ONLY TWENTY-SEVEN, BUT HE HAS been all over the world. His travels have taken him to Mexico, Costa Rica, Honduras, Taiwan, mainland China, the Philippines, Thailand, Malaysia, Singapore, India, and Indonesia. He has taught adults and teenagers, but now his pupils are three- to six-year-olds in a Montessori preschool. He loves children of this age. If he's having a bad day, the kids find a way to lift his spirits. David's friends know him as the guy who often comes up with a weird idea for something fun to do. One favorite is a midnight hike on a mountain trail. His philosophy is one of tolerance and love for others.

5 DAVID—
From World Traveler
to Preschool Teacher

I HAD A HAPPY CHILDHOOD, A GOOD HOME, AND lots of friends. But my father's death from a heart attack at age thirty-four shattered some of that happiness. I was seven and my older brother, Joe, was nine.

Joe is a high-energy guy. Like anyone else, he can use his energy for good or direct it negatively. My father's death hit Joe hard. For the next several years he had a lot of *negative* energy. As the result of getting into drugs and alcohol, he had to live away from home for two years. That affected the whole family. He had the "bad boy" label, so I took on the role of the good boy. Finally, in his twenties, Joe was able to turn everything around. He's married now and has a nice wife. My mom thinks the positive influences in his early years helped. First he became a chef and trained in New York. Now he's a massage therapist and makes a good income.

I went to a small private college and majored in

psychology. I also took lots of Spanish courses. I'm half Spanish, on my mom's side. I was an exchange student in Mexico for four months during my junior year. After college, I participated in another exchange program, this time living in Costa Rica for sixteen months. When I came back to the United States, I had no trouble getting a job. I worked as a substance abuse counselor at Servicios de la Raza, a social service agency.

Then the travel bug bit again. I'm not sure if I can put my goal into words. I guess I wanted to broaden my view of life and to experience different cultures. I wanted to go beyond the comfort level I have in this country. One advantage of being single is that you can take off for anywhere on a moment's notice. One night a friend and I decided to go to Taiwan. Almost immediately we were on our way. The traveling I did made me more aware of my own culture and helped me grow in my understanding of myself and others. It made me want to see more of the world.

I returned to the United States in December of 1993 and got a job teaching preschoolers. I really like kids of this age and have no plans to change careers right now.

I'm currently living with my mom in the house in which I grew up. I don't have a girlfriend right now, so why not? We share household duties and expenses. My mother teaches toddlers in a center for young children.

Swimming, hiking, biking, and playing basketball are some of the things I like to do. I like being active and getting together with friends. I read novels or books about the education of children.

Professionally, I want to be the best teacher I can be. Personally, I'm working on self-discipline and being in control of my emotions. I don't want to yell at a kid even if he makes me mad. My main personal goal is to grow in love and understanding.

I imagine I'll be a father someday. Maybe in my early thirties. Two or three kids would be enough.

Older men make better fathers. A young man goes through a lot of changes in his early twenties. As you get older, you find out more about the person you are. You discover what works and what doesn't work.

I think that by postponing parenthood you have a chance to explore more of life. You can act on the things you want to do more freely. You can discover more of the possibilities the world has to offer. After that, you may be more ready to settle down.

MATT IS A YOUNG DOCTOR, AGE TWENTY- six. This year he graduated from medical school and began his training in psychiatry. The oldest of three children, Matt is very close to his family. His mother, father, and two sisters are all involved in the helping professions. His father is a pediatrician (children's doctor). His mother is a pediatric nurse. One sister is studying social work, and the other sister wants to be a physical thera- pist. Although Matt is not yet engaged, he has a serious girlfriend, three years older than him. She is also a doctor. He talks about the important people in his life and how he arrived at his career decisions.

6 MATT— Goals: Marriage and Fatherhood

I USED TO BELIEVE THAT THINGS WORKED OUT FOR the best no matter what. I'm not sure about that anymore. People need a little help.

In my junior year of high school I went into a sort of slump. I was obsessed with one girl, but she paid no attention to me. I finally got disgusted with myself and started doing more. I joined the mountaineering club and became president of the cultural exchange club. I forced myself to be more outgoing about making friends and trying new things. I got involved.

Mentors and teachers were important for me too. In my senior year of high school, I had two motivating teachers, in Spanish and physics. They helped me focus on learning for its own sake, not just for grades. I got more interested in my classes and figured out ways to make them fun.

Applying to colleges was stressful. I hated writing all those essays about myself. But my parents kept pushing. If they hadn't, I might never have

Talk to older males when you are confused about life's many difficult choices.

sent the applications. In my second year of medical school, a professor turned me on to the field of psychiatry. I liked the idea of helping a person try to enjoy and cope with life. It's more than just medicine. I adjusted my schedule and spent some time working with patients in the state hospital. I liked medical school because I began to see a reason for what I was learning.

Maybe being the oldest in a family makes a person overly responsible. But I think it's good to have goals—some things you're good at or are trying to be good at. You achieve those goals and then you're ready to move on to the next stage. Right now a lot of my friends are making the change from educational and career goals to an emphasis on marriage or long-term relationships.

In the last few years, I've had a strong sense of what I wanted to do. I put those goals first. Financial stability is important. A person has to have a steady source of income. Then marriage. I used to date for the fun of it. Now I look at the person I'm going with as a possible marriage partner. If a relationship doesn't have the possibility of marriage, I get out. Fatherhood is high on my list. I think one of the main purposes of marriage is to have kids. I think I'll be ready to be a father in three or four years.

I'm amazed that my parents already had kids when they were my age. As I was growing up, though, I felt a lot of pressure *not* to have kids. I had one scare: A girl I was dating thought she might be pregnant. As things turned out, she wasn't. That was good because I wasn't ready (emotionally or financially) to be a father at twenty-one. And I didn't want to marry her.

In general, I think older fathers make better fathers. When I compare myself now to the way I was years ago, I feel I've changed a lot. I'm more stable. I've had five more years of living with various roommates. I've had to do a lot of problem-solving; for example, making chore lists and dividing up the bills. In my relationships, I've had more experience at working things out.

KHOA, THIRTY-SIX, IS A SCHOOL SOCIAL worker. Someday he hopes to become an elementary school principal. When he was seventeen years old, he escaped from Vietnam with his mother and father. Two of his brothers were killed in the Vietnam War. Two sisters and one brother still live in that country; Khoa has not seen them for twenty years. He enjoys working with children, especially those of Asian heritage. He wants to help them cope with the challenges of a society that is new and sometimes overwhelming for them.

7 KHOA— Making a Life in a New Land

I WAS BORN IN VIETNAM. MY FATHER WAS AN
accountant who worked for the U.S. government.
My mother was a social worker. I had seven older
brothers and sisters. We were well-off financially,
and life was good.

Then came the war. My oldest brother, thirty-
four years old at the time, was an army doctor. He
was killed in the war. My twenty-one-year-old
brother, a medical student, was also killed in the
war. The rest of us had to flee for our lives. On
April 30, 1975, my mother, father, and I set off for
America in a small boat. We had to leave everything behind and start over again with nothing.

For a short time, all three of us lived with our
sponsors, a family with kids my age. Then my parents got a small apartment. I stayed with the
American family to learn English. Every night for
hours I drilled myself on the language. It was my
last year of high school. The adjustment was hard.
I felt like an outsider both in the family and at

school. The customs were so different: for example, the way the kids talked to their parents.

After high school, I attended a community college and worked as a dishwasher. At times I also worked in the library and the communications lab. Upon finishing school, I was proud to be listed in *Who's Who in American Junior Colleges*. From there I went on to a university, where, after two more years, I got my bachelor's degree in psychology and French.

While in college, I went to France for a semester as an exchange student. In Paris, I met the person who was to become my wife—although I didn't know it then. Her name was Thai; she was also Vietnamese. She was five years older than me, and worked as a chef. During the next several years, I found ways to get back to Paris to see her. I even worked as her restaurant manager for six months.

When I was a kid, I always saw myself as a lawyer. But my experiences as a refugee led me toward the vocation of social work. I entered a graduate program in social work in 1985. In 1989, Thai was able to come to the United States and become my wife.

By this time, I was thirty and she was thirty-five. We wanted to have a child, but we wanted Thai to be able to stay at home with the child. We didn't want to be two working parents. As a result, we struggle with finances, but we believe it's important to have one parent at home full time. In Vietnam parents are teachers. They impart values of social responsibility to their children. Our Buddhist religion emphasizes respect, wisdom, and compassion for others. Our son Louis is now in a public school in kindergarten.

For me, it's important to have goals. I still wish I could have become an attorney, but I didn't have the money. Now I'd like to get my Ph.D. in education. My personal goals are to have a good family life, to play some tennis, and to go back to Vietnam someday to do something to help my people.

As a younger man, I never felt any pressure to have children. I'm glad I waited until I had a career and a decent income. Between thirty and thirty-five is a perfect time, I think, for most people to have a family. I tell the young people I work with to wait. They need to get more experience, confidence, and money. I tell them to experience life for a while and to enjoy themselves before taking on too many responsibilities and commitments.

People should be grateful for the opportunity to live in the United States. Here they have plenty of chances. I tell young people this: "You can grow and be successful. It's not going to be easy. But if you commit to hard work, you can meet your goals."

GREGORY, TWENTY-FIVE, GOT HIS FIRST JOB delivering newspapers at age nine. He kept that job for five years. At fourteen he began working as a dishwasher in a Mexican-food restaurant. After that, he worked in fast-food restaurants for many years. His jobs in the restaurant business paved the way to his current career as a public health sanitarian. Gregory's mother and grandparents raised him, but he gives much additional credit for his success in life to his uncle Larry.

8 GREGORY— Guardian of Health

MY UNCLE PROVIDED A POSITIVE ROLE MODEL FOR me. I idolized him. Because of his intelligence, he earned the respect of those around him. He was smart and quiet, a kind and very cool person.

My dad served in Vietnam, and my mother worked as a secretary for the federal government. They were both twenty-one years old when I was born. Three years later, they got divorced.

My college years were interesting. I ended up at Northland College in Ashland, Wisconsin. I think they recruited me because of my test scores, which were in the top 3 percent of minorities nationwide. The school is about a mile from Lake Superior on a wooded campus. What's interesting is that I was never an outdoor person. But in college I was able to go camping, fishing, scuba diving, and sea kayaking. I welcomed those experiences and discovered a whole new world. I volunteered for the Search and Rescue Team and served as team leader in my sophomore year. In my senior year I played basketball. My degree is in biology. My major interests were fisheries and wildlife and entomology, the study of insects.

After graduation, I worked as an environmental chemist in private industry. In 1992, I applied for my current job with the city health department, although I didn't expect to get it. The job involves inspecting restaurants and responding to complaints. Our goal is to decrease the amount of food-borne disease. We come up with a reasonable explanation in 90 percent of cases, which makes correction possible.

Besides work, I play basketball and softball and go bowling and swimming. I like to play board games, too, like chess, Monopoly, and Battletech. Sometimes I've played in tournaments.

When I was a kid, I wanted to be a pilot. At about sixteen, I went to aviation ground school and got high school credits. You learn the principles of flying, how to make calculations, the science of weather, and other things related to flying. I never became a pilot because of the expense, but I haven't given up on the dream. I'm going back to aviation school two evenings a week. I still want to fly a plane, maybe professionally.

I've had a serious girlfriend for about two years. She works for the health department too, but we met in high school. Then we met again when I was inspecting a restaurant. She was buying some take-out food. We started talking and, gradually, became friendly.

I'd like to get married in a couple of years, and yes, she could be the one. I used to think I could be a father sometime between the ages of twenty-seven and thirty. But now that I'm twenty-five, it's looking more and more like thirty. I don't feel I'm emotionally ready yet. I still don't have enough patience.

My main goal is to be successful in life and work for my own *personal* satisfaction. To me, being happy in your job and life is more important than making lots of money. You can always make more money, but not everyone can live a happy life.

DON, TWENTY-EIGHT, AND HIS WIFE JEANENE
met ten years ago during their first year of
college. When he was a junior, Don applied
for an internship with the federal government.
He didn't get it and was very disappointed.
But some things work out for the best.
Because Don didn't move away, he and
Jeanene became better acquainted. Two years
ago, they got married.

9 DON— Settling into Small Business

BESIDES MY PARENTS, THE PERSON WHO MOST changed my life was a Catholic brother. His name is Felix. He's a person who has dedicated his life to helping others. He's a friend of our family and was like an uncle to me. He took me on trips to the mountains and to the opera and symphony—things I couldn't have, and wouldn't have, done on my own. He taught me that it's okay for a man to hug the people he loves. To this day, I give my parents hugs and tell them I love them.

During my teenage years, I was like an only child. My brother David, who is six years older, left home at eighteen. By this time, Dad had finished college and had more time for me. When my brother was young, Dad was really busy with school and work. David became the rebel of the family. I saw a lot of the problems he had and tried to avoid them. He got married early and divorced. Now he's happily married and has three girls—five, four, and one. I get to practice parenting on my three nieces.

It is often not until they are older that people are ready for a committed relationship with one person.

In college I got a degree in political science. But for the past six years, I've been managing a bicycle shop. I've learned how to run a small business. Now my dad, my brother, and I are opening our own business, a travel agency. I like to travel and I like sports, so I thought of combining the two. Our specialty will be arranging trips for sports teams.

In high school my thoughts were on sports, not on girls. I still thought a lot about teen pregnancy. Many times it results from a lack of planning. Urges take over and one thing leads to another, sometimes to a baby. I didn't want to have kids until I could support them.

We have two dogs. They're our children right

now. Eventually, two kids would be fine—maybe in two or three years. But we want to enjoy each other for a while. We made this decision together. We like doing simple things like going to the movies or out to dinner, taking walks or biking, or going shopping. We can go on the spur of the moment. Our friends with kids are tied down, and most of them aren't even married yet.

One of our biggest adjustments was dealing with two sets of parents. Our families both live in town. Sometimes we solve what to do on holidays by having dinner at one place and dessert at the other.

I think older fathers make better fathers. They have had a chance to live a little and get some things out of their system. They have a greater understanding of life. They are generally more mellow and willing to assume the many responsibilities of fatherhood.

I have no desire to be rich or famous. I'm happy with my life and the way it's turned out so far. No second or third marriages for me. I hope to grow old with the one I love.

DAVID IS A KIND MAN WHO REMINDS SOME people of a teddy bear. He has Native American heritage through his father. His father rejected this heritage, but David has embraced it. Recently David became a father through adoption. Sometimes he has trouble believing how much his life has changed in the past year.

10 DAVID— Celebrating Heritage

I'M THE YOUNGEST OF THREE CHILDREN. MY TWO sisters were twelve and eleven years older, so I was like an only child. When I was about a year old, my father left the family. After the divorce, my mother had to support all of us. Because she was so busy, I was left to entertain myself. I spent my happiest hours alone, hiking in the hills behind our house. I also enjoyed watching the trains go by.

Both of my parents drank a lot. I saw enough of alcoholism to turn me off. Besides, I'm a Sundancer, which means I've made a commitment to abstain from alcohol and drugs.

Five years ago, I met Jonette at a powwow. Although she's not Native American, she had gotten interested in American Indian rituals. Through participating in the same activities, we became friends. Eventually we got married.

Jonette has always been interested in adoption. I wasn't so sure, but one night I said, "Let's go for it." There are so many older children in need of families. Most people want a baby, but I didn't care if I never had to change a diaper.

Working at a copy store, I don't make a whole lot of money. Sometimes I feel I'm still too young to be a father. But before we got our kids, we took parenting classes and adoption classes. We read about fifty books on those subjects.

Last April, Travis, six, and Spencer, five, moved in with us. Their heritage is Ogalala Sioux—like mine. Jonette and I expect them to participate in powwows along with us and the other kids their age. We hope they'll like native dancing as much as we do. If not, that's okay. We want to give them the opportunity to be best they can be, however that turns out. We'll just have to wait and see.

Epilogue

YOU'VE HEARD FROM TEN YOUNG MEN WHO HAVE chosen not to become fathers at an early age. Their hopes and dreams include such activities as backpacking in Nepal, becoming a pilot or a business owner, competing in the Olympics, or getting a college degree.

In addition to planning for the future, they're enjoying life in the present: raising and racing horses; playing hockey, pool, tennis, and basketball; going camping, country-western dancing, or scuba diving; playing drums in a rock band; going out to dinner and the movies.

Most of them want to become fathers someday. But they're in no hurry. By delaying parenthood for a while, these men believe they'll be ready for the responsibility. David and Khoa explain why waiting to become dads was the best choice for them.

Do you share any of the interests and dreams of the men you've read about? What are your own hopes for the future? Do they include a college degree or an exciting career? Think about what you need to do to reach your goals. As you have seen throughout this book, anything is possible if you set your mind to it. Be fair to yourself and give yourself the opportunity to succeed. You deserve it!

Glossary

accountant A person who deals with financial records.

anthology A collection of literary works, such as poems or short stories.

attorney Attorney-at-law; a lawyer.

ethics The study of morals and choices to be made between right and wrong.

mare A female horse.

mentor A respected teacher or counselor or any person who has served as a role model to another (usually younger) person.

microbiology The science of microscopic plants and animals.

Montessori preschool A school for young children that stresses the development of the child's own motivation. Maria Montessori was an Italian doctor and educator.

Navajo A Native American people whose reservation covers parts of Arizona, New Mexico, and Utah.

pediatrics The branch of medicine dealing with children.

peer A person of equal rank, age, or class.

Ph.D. A doctor of philosophy.

philosophy The study of the natural laws underlying reality.

physical therapist A person who treats injury by mechanical means, such as exercise, heat, and massage.

political science The study of government and politics.

psychiatrist A doctor who specializes in the mental health of patients.

psychology The study of behavior.

social worker A person who works to improve social welfare.

stallion An adult male horse that can breed.

substance abuse The destructive use of harmful drugs and alcohol.

triathlon An endurance race involving three sports, usually swimming, cycling, and running.

Help List

Advocates for Youth
1025 Vermont Avenue, NW, Suite 200
Washington, DC 20005
(202) 347-5700

Big Brothers Big Sisters of America
230 North 13th Street
Philadelphia, PA 19107
(215) 567-7000
e-mail: bbbsa@aol.com
Web site: http://www.bbbsa.org

National Center on Fathers and Families
Box 58
3700 Walnut Street
Philadelphia, PA 19104-6216
(215) 573-5500
e-mail: gadsden@literacy.upenn.edu

National Institute for Responsible Fatherhood
8555 Hough Avenue
Cleveland, OH 44106
(216) 791-1468

National Parenting Center
22801 Ventura Boulevard, Suite 110
Woodlands Hills, CA 91367
(818) 225-8990
Web site: http://www.tnpc.com

Planned Parenthood Federation of America
810 Seventh Avenue
New York, NY 10019
(212) 541-7800
e-mail: communications@ppfa.org
Web site: http://www.ppfa.org/ppfa/

In Canada:

Planned Parenthood Federation of Canada
1 Nicholas Street, Suite 430
Ottawa, Ontario K1N 7B7
(613) 241-4474

For Further Reading

Ayer, Eleanor. *Everything You Need to Know About Teen Fatherhood*. New York: The Rosen Publishing Group, 1993.

Berlfein, Judy. *Teen Pregnancy*. San Diego, CA: Lucent Books, 1992.

Bode, Janet. *Kids Having Kids: People Talk About Teen Pregnancy*. New York: Franklin Watts, 1992.

Dash, Leon. *When Children Want Children: An Inside Look at the Crisis of Teenage Parenthood*. New York: Viking-Penguin, 1990.

Gravelle, Karen, and Peterson, Leslie. *Teenage Fathers*. New York: Julian Messner, 1992.

Kuklin, Susan. *What Do I Do Now? Talking About Teenage Pregnancy*. New York: G. P. Putnam's Sons, 1991.

Lindsay, Jeanne. *Teenage Marriage: Coping with Reality*. Buena Park, CA: Morning Glory Press, 1988.

———. *Teen Dads: Rights, Responsibilities and Joys*. Buena Park, CA: Morning Glory Press, 1993.

————. *Teens Look at Marriage: Rainbows, Roles, and Reality.* Buena Park, CA: Morning Glory Press, 1985.

Meier, Gisela. *Teenage Pregnancy.* North Bellmore, NY: Marshall Cavendish, 1994.

Robinson, Bryan. *Teenage Fathers.* New York: The Free Press, 1987.

Rozakis, Laurie. *Teen Pregnancy: Why Are Kids Having Babies?* New York: Twenty-First Century Books, 1993.

Index

About the Author

Barbara Moe is a nurse, social worker, and freelance writer who loves working with young people and helping them face challenges. She lives in Colorado.

Photo Credits

Cover by Guillermina de Ferrari; p. 16 by Matthew Baumann and Kim Sonsky; pp. 18, 22 by Kim Sonsky; p. 20 © Steve Skjold Photographs; p. 36 by Maria Moreno; p. 48 © International Stock/Alain McLaughlin; p. 52 by Yung-Hee Chia. All other photos by Guillermina de Ferrari.

Layout and Design

Erin McKenna